Eskimos

Contents

Eskimos

Kate Petty

Illustrated by
Maurice Wilson

small  world

Gloucester Press
New York · London · Toronto · Sydney

People of the Arctic

The Eskimos are the people of the Arctic. They call themselves the Inuit. The lands they live in are some of the coldest parts of eastern Russia, North America, Canada and Greenland.

Very little grows in the snow and ice.
No trees grow that far north.
The Eskimos lived a wandering life so
that they could find the food that
would keep them alive at the
different times of the year. They put
up new homes wherever they stopped.

Map showing where Eskimos live

Decorated window coverings were made from seals' bladders

Eskimo homes

The Eskimo word for somewhere to live is "igloo." In winter the Eskimos built homes from earth and stone. In summer they lived in tents made from animal skins.

Eskimos on hunting trips built their igloos from blocks cut from the snow. They built up the blocks in a spiral. The entrance was a tunnel under the snow. Lamps that burned animal fat gave them light and warmth.

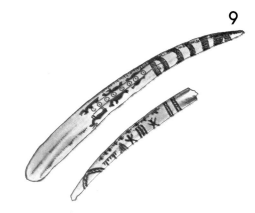

Decorated ivory knives

Some Eskimos still build snow houses like this

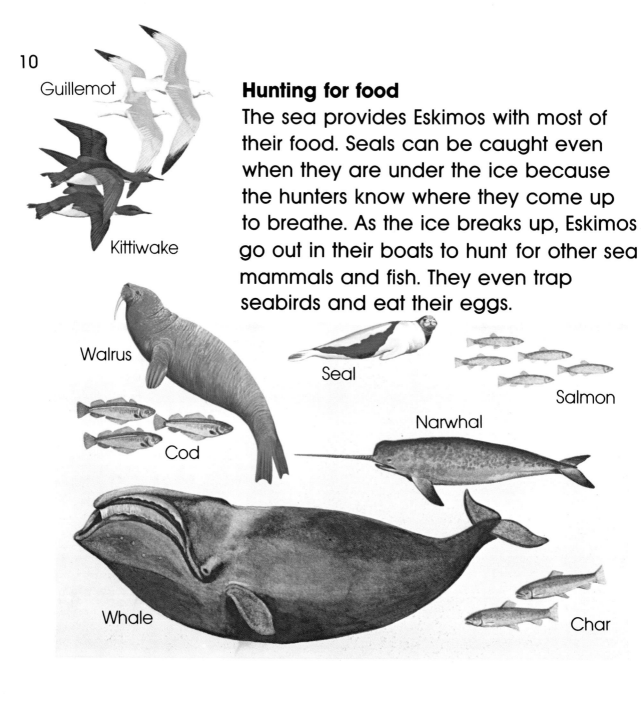

Guillemot

Kittiwake

Hunting for food

The sea provides Eskimos with most of their food. Seals can be caught even when they are under the ice because the hunters know where they come up to breathe. As the ice breaks up, Eskimos go out in their boats to hunt for other sea mammals and fish. They even trap seabirds and eat their eggs.

Walrus

Seal

Salmon

Cod

Narwhal

Whale

Char

There are also polar bears, foxes and hares to be hunted. In summer some Eskimos go inland to find the herds of caribou. Geese and more fish are found in the rivers then and there are many kinds of berries to be picked.

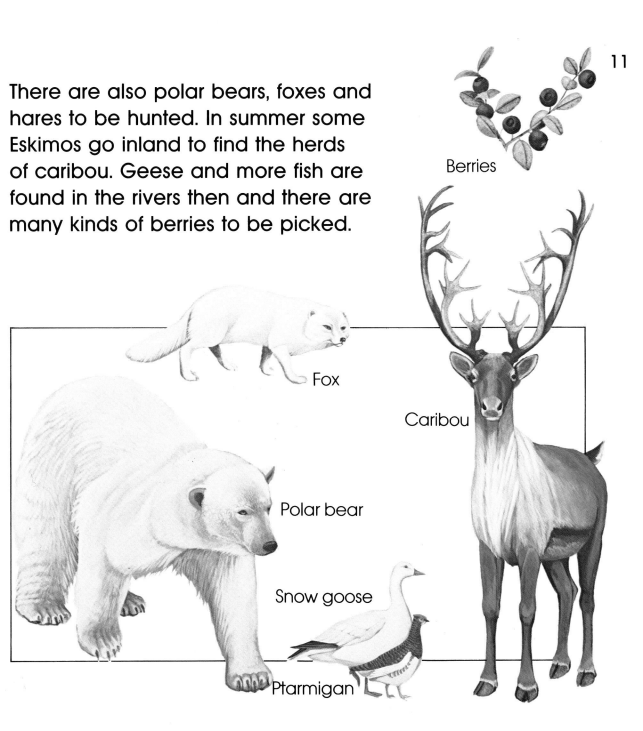

Berries

Fox

Caribou

Polar bear

Snow goose

Ptarmigan

Sleds and boats

Sleds were pulled across the snow and ice by dogs.
The sleds were made from wood and bone.

The smooth surface
of the runners
was molded from mud,
and then brushed with
water which froze
to a glassy finish.

This Umiak is a large boat for carrying cargo.
The women usually did the rowing.
Umiaks were also used for hunting whales.

This one-seater Kayak
is made from sealskin
stretched over a
frame of bone
or driftwood.

Waiting for the whale

Whales are still hunted by the Alaskan Eskimos.
One whale can provide a large amount of food.
Whale hunters work as a team.

Sealskins filled
with air are tied
to the harpoon tips.
They slow the whale
down once it
is struck.

The boats are launched when the first whale is
sighted. The hunters use harpoons to wound the
whale. When it is dead they tow it to the
shore.

The useful caribou

Caribou are like reindeer. Eskimos who live inland depend on caribou for food, skins and fat for fuel.

In spring and fall caribou cross the tundra in huge herds of up to 100,000 animals. The Eskimos drive them into the water to catch them.

Eskimos string the fish to lines held in their mouths

Summer fishing

In summer salmon swim up the river
from the sea. Eskimos build dams to trap them
and wade waist-deep into the water to spear
them with three-pronged harpoons.

Knife for cutting
skins

A use for everything

Everyone helps when a whale has been
killed. Eskimos eat little bits as
they work. The useful blubber is cut
in large blocks. It will be used as
fuel for lighting and cooking.

Scrapers

Bones, ivory and horns from animals were used in building boats and sleds, tools, weapons and even toys. Skins were the only materials the Eskimos had for making tents, clothes and blankets.

Skins being scraped clean before being sewn with animal sinews. This woman chews a skin to soften it.

This Canadian Eskimo hunter is wearing the original hooded parka, made from sealskins. A fox tail sewn around the tops of his boots keeps the snow out. An Alaskan hunter wore a layer of grass or moss between his socks and boots to keep his feet warm.

Warm clothes

Eskimos have to wear warm clothes or the cold will kill them. These were always made from loose layers of skins. The soft fur or feathers of the inner layer were worn next to the skin. Different styles were worn in different places.

Snow goggles cut down the glare of the bright snow

A Greenland woman

A jacket of eiderduck feathers

A woman wearing sealskin clothing

A test of strength

Spearing the bone with
the pin trains the eye
as well as being fun

This game
is called
nuglutang

Time to play

Children who were too young to join in the hard work had plenty of time to play. In the fall, with food stored away for the winter, everyone had a chance to relax. Eskimos held feasts, with singing and dancing and storytelling.

The walrus skin stretched out for a game of "skin toss" is rather like a trampoline. Children see who can jump the highest.

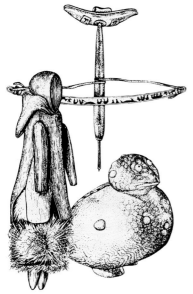

Eskimo crafts

Eskimos made all their own tools for cutting and carving and drilling. In their spare time they carved many beautiful objects from bone, ivory and wood. Some people still know how to make holes with a bow drill, which is held in the mouth.

A bow drill was made from ivory

The doll and the bird are made from wood

The whale is carved from a narwhal tusk

The mask and the picture show you how the Eskimos painted and drew. Masks were worn for dancing. People are dancing and drumming in the picture below.

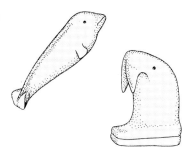

These little charms were worn to bring good luck

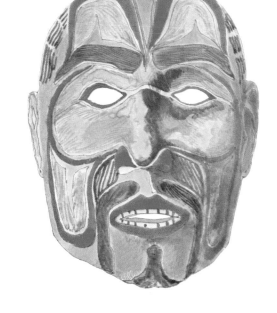

Modern life in the Arctic

Eskimos are no longer cut off from the rest of
the world by snow and ice. People from other
countries are interested in the oil and minerals
to be found in the Arctic. Now most Eskimos
live in settlements with stores and schools.
The children are learning a new way of life, but
they still remember their old traditions.

Index